YOUR KNOWLEDGE HAS VALUE

Raymond Cook

Business Plan for Setting Up a Shop Selling Genetically Modified Food

GRIN Verlag

Bibliografische Information der Deutschen Nationalbibliothek:

Die Deutsche Bibliothek verzeichnet diese Publikation in der Deutschen National-
bibliografie; detaillierte bibliografische Daten sind im Internet über http://dnb.d-
nb.de/ abrufbar.

Imprint:

Copyright © 2011 GRIN Verlag GmbH
Druck und Bindung: Books on Demand GmbH, Norderstedt Germany
ISBN: 978-3-656-44319-3

GRIN - Your knowledge has value

Der GRIN Verlag publiziert seit 1998 wissenschaftliche Arbeiten von Studenten, Hochschullehrern und anderen Akademikern als eBook und gedrucktes Buch. Die Verlagswebsite www.grin.com ist die ideale Plattform zur Veröffentlichung von Hausarbeiten, Abschlussarbeiten, wissenschaftlichen Aufsätzen, Dissertationen und Fachbüchern.

Visit us on the internet:

http://www.grin.com/

http://www.facebook.com/grincom

http://www.twitter.com/grin_com

BUSINESS PLAN FOR SETTING UP A SHOP SELLING

GENETICALLY MODIFIED FOODS

Genemod shop business plan

Table of Contents

1.0 Executive summary

Genemod Shop is a company whose ideas of formation dates back to October 2010, when four undergraduate students taking accounting, horticulture, marketing and business management engaged in an entrepreneurial discussion. Scheduled to start its operations in May 2011, its main purpose is to provide quality and timely food to students the University of reading. It will provide Purple tomatoes, British blackcurrant berries, Tomato puree and some GM vegetables as the main GM food. The name Genemod was arrived at after considering many options one being the combination of Genetic and Modified to get Genemod hence the company name. On the market opportunity, with the current trend in food consumption, it has been realized that genetically modified food remains the best option both at home and commercial residents. Students in the university travel to the supermarkets to get food which should be availed near their halls of residents. The university has many halls of resident including student village, hillside court, Martindale court and Mackinder hall among others which represents a good market to be exploited.

The company seeks a capital of £10,000 for the start up. This will be raised from member's contributions, loan from financial institution and venture capitalists' contributions. Repayment of the loan will begin immediately within two months of its operations. The shop faces competition from two main suppliers who bring fruits and vegetables to the school compound on Mondays and Wednesdays. Some students go to the supermarkets to buy the food hence this constitutes another competitor.

2.0 Current situation and market analysis

The current economic crisis all over the world calls for interventions in food production and distribution. Many students are paying extra coins for buying food from supermarkets and distributors who come to the university twice a week. Sometimes there is a shortage of food that leads to using unbalanced diet and cooking of meals without some ingredients like tomatoes. Analysis is the key to determining the potential profitability of a business and expected rate of return on investment (Stevens, 1993, P. 9). Market analysis done involves identifying competitors, current and growth potentials. Market segmentation will be done from the basis. This portion of the plan will also identify target customers who are the prospects of our food products.

2.1 Industry analysis

The main suppliers of the genetically modified food come to the university on Mondays and Thursdays to sell their products. The sellers purchase food products from accredited suppliers who give them quantity discounts and after sale services like transportation to the university. Another main competitor is the supermarket in the town where students go for their food products. It stocks different kinds of food but it is opposed to the idea of genetically modified food. The supermarkets sale hybrid food products at slightly higher price compared to genetically modified food. This is justified by the fact that they take a lot of time to mature. Students go there since most of the time they don't have an option when the semi weekly suppliers delays.

2.2 SWOT analysis

After analyzing the food industry in which the company will operate and more specifically selling genetically modified food to students, the following were identified. Strengths included quality of food products to be stocked, differentiation from competitors, good customer services and convenient location of the shop. High quality from accredited suppliers which will be enhanced by mode of packaging will differentiate the product from the competitors hence make Genemod the best food distributor in the university. The Weaknesses included the fact that the owners are inexperienced in terms of business as they are students who have not been involved much in business. Genetically modified food is a new product where students have only learnt hence lack of experience in handling the same.

However it has opportunities to educate students on quality of genetically modified food and establish a relationship with school administration to assist in marketing of the products. This will be done through using the school website more especially under the links of accommodation to communicate to students on the days the food will be availed in school. The threats include: Miscalculation of customer tests and preferences where the company anticipates that many students will prefer genetically modified food to hybrid one. This might not be the case but the company hope for the best. Another problem is the timing of food distribution as there might be examination when the company distributes food. This will make the company suspend its operations hence poor reputation. This will be countered through employing two people to do the same work during examination time.

3.0 Products

After market analysis, there was a need to bring products into the market to fill the gap that exists. Genemod will stock quality food that is unique all over the University Of reading. The brand names given will be patented and will make them hard to copy. The quality of the food will be enhanced by mode of packaging, structure and its design. The brands given will be familiarized through Television, poster, decorated van, university website, facebook and billboards across the university.

3.1 Product assortment
Purple tomatoes

They are developed in higher biotic compound hence can help people who do not eat 5 portions of fruits and vegetable a day as recommended. Purple tomato has antioxidant pigment which has ant-cancer property and has significantly longer life span. It also has anti-inflammatory properties that help in boosting eyesight and it is known to prevent obesity and diabetes. Some concerns have been raised about this found but they will be addressed accordingly through educating students about the importance the tomato as it uses modern technology. They will be told to try and compare with the previous food supplied (BBC News 2008:1).

British blackcurrant berries

It has anti-oxidant compound that help in preventing Alzheimer and cancer. It has the capability of preventing brain degeneration and age related diseases. Five fruits will be packaged and sold at £ 1.6, £ 0.2 higher than the normal price in the market. The higher price will be justified through the transportation costs involved and convenient to the customers.

Tomato puree

The tomato has its rooting gene removed and it last longer than conventionally grown tomatoes. It has a strong test and is cheaper as it requires less energy and water when growing. It is accepted in the UK market and common among students. It will be stocked in plenty and packaged in 500 grams and 1 kg tin. The selling price will be £ 1.3 and £ 2.5 respectively.

Cabbages, cauliflower, sprouts and broccoli

This will form the main vegetable sold by Genemod shop. The shop will be selling both white and purple sprouting in the category of broccoli. Spring, wither and summer cabbages will be availed during their respective seasons to ensure there is plenty of vegetables in the university. Cauliflower will be another important type of vegetable availed by the shop. They will be sold at an average price of £ 1.2 per kilogram.

Table 1 below summarizes the price of each commodity in by Genemod shop and competitors

Food name	Quantity	Price by Genemod (£)	Price by competitors (£)
Purple tomatoes	500 g	1.3	1.2
British blackcurrant berries	1 kg	1.6	1.4
Tomato puree	1 kg	1. 5	1.5
Cabbages	500 g	2.1	2.2
Broccoli	500 g	1.2	1.1
Cauliflower	2 kg	2.5	2.4

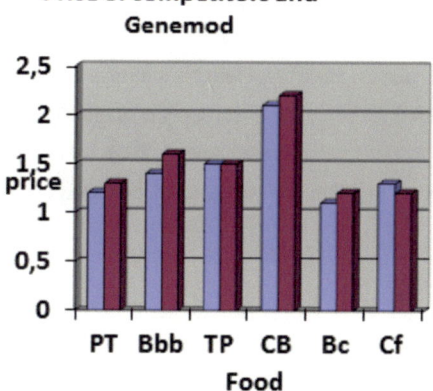

KEY
PT – *Purple tomato*
Bbb – *British blackcurrant berries*
TP- *Tomato Puree*
CB – *Cabbage*
Bc- *Broccoli*
Cf – *Cauliflower*

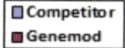

Taking the average price 1 kilogram of any product to be 1.8, the demand and supply curve will be represented as shown below.

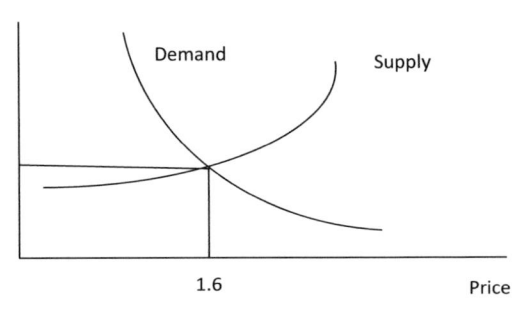

Demand	Supply	Price
500	190	1.1
400	220	1.2
350	250	1.2
330	280	1.4
300	320	1.6
280	380	1.7
250	420	1.8
220	480	1.9
210	500	2
200	520	2.1

3.2 Product sourcing, buying and inventory management.

The genetically modified food will be purchased from UK famers and government agencies growing the food. Different farmers will be contacted and prices be compared with quality. The shop will make an agreement with the suppliers to ensure stock is maintained up to date and during peak season when students require more, a lot will be supplied. The company will ensure that there is enough stock and through application of economic order quantity formula, we will minimize the total cost of stock (Hansen2006, p. 763). Inventory will also be monitored by inventory management and Point of sale system developed to serve the shop.

4.0 Organizational plan

The shop will be a small one hence no complication in management. After two years is when executive positions will be created as it will open up more branches within the UK market.

4.1 Hours of business

It will be supplying food to school on Mondays and Thursdays when most of the members have no lessons. The supply will take place from 12 am to 8 pm when most students will be preparing meals. The date was also arrived at since the other suppliers bring the food on Saturdays and Sundays.

4.2 Company ownership

Genemod will be formed as a private limited company with the owners being four undergraduate students working interchangeably. Two university interns will be employed to assist in bringing the food and disturbing to those clients who may request for delivery. One casual will be employed to do extensive marketing and report on any need that may arise.

4.3. Company location

It is important for every business owner to figure out how location will contribute to the success of their business (Pakroo 2008, p. 50). The right location for Genemod to succeed is outside Mackinder Hall of residence. However this will be achieved after one year since it will operate from outside as the supply will be done twice a week. Then after that, the profit made will be used to rent a place and start the business of selling the GM food daily.

4.4 Start up

Genemod will open May 2011, five months from now. The start up expenses is estimated to be £ 10,000. The capital is required to help in running costs for 1 year after which it would have reached breakeven point. The set up costs will be finance by owners' contribution and finance from venture capitalists.

5.0 Marketing approach

Kloper et al (2006) talks of the four Ps that can be used to market an idea. The first P stands for a physical product or service and other aspects of the product such as the brand name that the company gives. Genetically modified food is the product to be sold. They will be packaged and given brand names with patents to make them hard to copy by competitors. Other aspects of the product will include quality, packaging, attractive appearance, customer assurance, and site effect description of the food. This will provide the customers with credible information and the credibility of the company will go high. The food will be packaged in different quantities from 50 grams to 2 kilograms.

Another P stands for the price at which the customers will be charged. This will demonstrate the product's worthiness for the customers. Pricing will be based on the total cost of acquiring plus 30% markup. There will be lists price, volume discounts, financing and allowances given. Prices will be tagged on each package sample and on the shop website. The prices will be slightly higher from those in other shops since customers will be assured of the better quality associated with price. It will be justified through educating them on the superior technology in food production and they will always receive best. Another justification for high prices will be the fact that the business starting and operational expenses are high. The place, the third P, is where the product is distributed and made available for sale. It also includes the quality and quantity of the food sold. Food will be availed in the required place at the right time hence satisfying customer needs.

Lastly, promotion is the means of informing, reminding and persuading customers about the offers. The company will employ pulling and pushing promotional strategies. In pulling strategy, Genemod shop will stimulate final user demand through advertising and sales promotion (Kurtz 2007 p. 488). Others will include use of School magazines, internet and school website. Students will also be informed through billboards, leaflets and facebook. Pulling strategy will rely more heavily on personal selling, trade discounts and door to door campaign on the importance of using genetically modified food.

6.0 Operational plan and supply chain

The operational plan summarizes the major action programs and contains: objectives, program description, responsibility assignment and resource needs (Shim 2009, p. 30). It is concerned with short term activities of the business. The main marketing objective is to increase awareness through product education, communication and extensive marketing.

6.1 Sales strategy

The company will offer personalized customer service by knowledgeable employees, students, who will attend to individual needs and differences. This will develop customer relationships and royalty that makes customers return for the products. Through the use of shop management system and point of sale software to record customers' information, the company will make follow ups with mails and phone calls for special events and encourage customers to give us suggestions on any new product that they may want.

6.2 Market segmentation

The shop's major customer target is the students in the University of reading. Demographic segment will form a major basis in the marketing of the shop's products. Female students like more fruits than man according a survey conducted. They would like purchasing products with feminine appearance and brands. The packages for their products will contain pictures of ladies enjoying meals prepared by genetically modified ingredients. For men, they want to be assured of more energy hence some products will be packaged in containers of people in a gym. Other products will be general for anybody to buy. Another basis of segmentation will be halls of resident served. There are many halls but the company will consider putting up its shop outside Mackinder hall, a new hall opened October last year with 562 en suit rooms, as from next year.

7.0 Management plan

7.1 Ownership structure

The business will be a private limited company with the four founders being the managers. The first member who is doing studying bachelor of business management will be responsible for the weekly operations of the shop. He will ensure semi weekly supplies are adhered to and legal procedures are followed. The second member is an accounting student and will be responsible in preparing financial statements and general financial report. He will give advice on financial matters and salary to all employees. The field of quality GM food will be monitored by a horticultural student who will ensure that farmers are contacted to supply quality products. Marketing will be done by the marketing student who will ensure that customers are reached and educated on the products. He will give advice on any marketing opportunity and strategies to put in place in order to increase the market share of the business.

The interns employed will be charged with the duty of supplying food to students' room and marketing the products. Sometimes they will assist in bringing the food from the suppliers using the company vehicle. They will report to the team member in charge of management and ensure that the shop operates smoothly. No responsibility is too big for anybody hence they can also advice on the management of the shop but they will not be involved in final decision making.

7.2 Legal requirements

The company will be registered under company registration act and fulfill all registration requirements. The law requires that we must not put ourselves, workers and the public in danger when operating any business. The high percentage of food retail through large supermarkets due to high standard requirements needed to supply that commodity (Mayes .. p. 2004). The company will maintain high standard hygiene and supply only approved products.

7.3 Personnel plan

To motivate each employ, the company will have to compensate its workers on services given. They will be paid according to the work they do and targets they meet. The interns will be paid amount to keep them coming but not entire salaries since they are in form of training. Table 2 below outlines the personnel needs for Genemod shop.

Job detail	Rate	Total
4 Managers	500	2000
Subordinate staff	300	300
2 Interns	150	300
Total		**2,600**

Chart showing compensation percantage of management, interns and subordinate

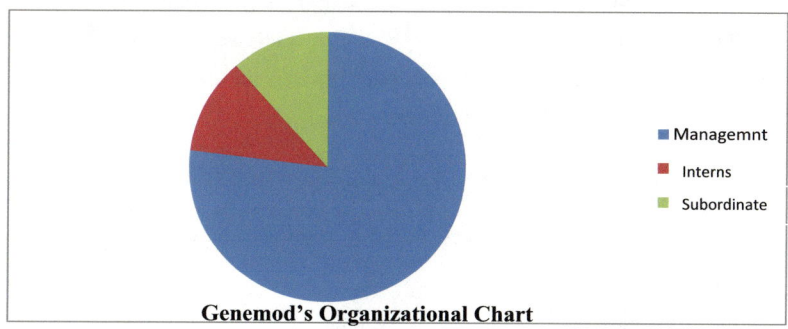

Genemod's Organizational Chart

8.0 Financial plan

The company will start by acquiring a loan from financial institution which will cover start-up expenses and the first six months of salary, taxes, and other petty expenses. Owner investment will be used to cover monthly cash flow shortages and inventory requirements which might not be anticipated. Other great contributors are venture capitalists, whom the plan is also going to be presented as they promised to give 20% of the capital. Profits will be reinvested so as to increase products and increase the number of personnel after the first year.

8.1 Financial assumptions

According to the information obtained from the government statistics website, the following are financial assumption. Economic growth is estimated to be 0.7% annually, business investment growth 3.1%, borrowing interest rate 4% and government tax rate 5% (UK National statistics 2010:1).

8.2 Estimated budget for one year

Table 3: Budget

Description	Amount (£)	Source of financing
Marketing	400	Owners contribution
General purchases	6,000	Owners contribution
Computer and software	500	Venture capitalists
Salaries and compensation	2,600	Loan from Bank
Contingencies	500	Venture capitalists
TOTAL	**10,000**	

8.3 Financial statements for the company

Profit and loss account

Revenue	15,000	15,000
Minus Cost of sales	**5,000**	
Gross profit	**10,000**	**10,000**
Operating costs		
Marketing	**400**	
Sales and distribution	**500**	
Administration costs	**2,600**	
Depreciation (Vehicle and other asset)	**400**	
Sob total		3,900
Pretax profit (Gross profit – operating costs)		**6,100**
Tax	**610**	
Net profit		5,490

Genemod shop

Balance sheet

For the year ended 31 Dec. 2011

Current assets		Capital	5,000
Stock	5,000	Long term Liabilities	
Debtors	3,000	Loan	3,500
Fixed assets		Current liabilities	
Vehicle	4,000	Creditors	5,500
	11,000		11,000

Cash flow statements

Cash received	15,000
Cash payments purchases	5,000
Cash paid to employees	2,600
Operating expenses	900
Taxes paid	610
Net cash	5,490

Financial ratios

Gross profit margin = gross profit/revenue

$$= 10,000/15,000$$

$$= 0.67$$

Net profit margin = net profit/revenue

$$= 5,490/15,000$$

$$= 0.37$$

Return on assets = net income / total assets

$$= 5,490/11,000$$

$$= 0.5$$

Rate of return on capital = net income/capita employed

$$= 5,490/10,000$$

$$= 0.549$$

Current ratio = current assets/current liabilities

$$= 8,000/5,500$$

$$= 1.45$$

Quick ratio = (current asset – inventory)/ current liabilities

$$= (8,000 – 6,000) / 5,500$$

$$= 2,000/5,500$$

= 0.36

Rate of stock turnover = average stock/ (cost of sales/365)

= average stock = 5,000/2 = 2,500

= 2,500/(5,000/365)

= 182.6

Break even analysis

After one, the total revenue would be 15,000 but the net profit will be 5,490. This means, it would have paid its creditors but servicing the loans. At the end of the third year, the business will finish paying its loans and expand more than three times from the first year.

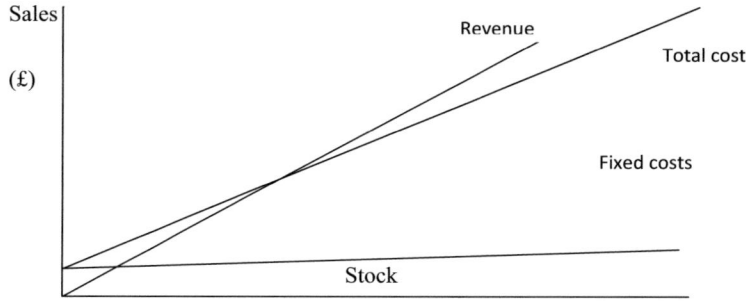

9.0 Growth plan investment

After one year, the company will open a shop at Mackinder halls café area. A shop would have then been opened there for the company to rent. This will make it double its profits and employ more people who are majorly students. On top of what the company would have achieved as profits, it will require an additional £ 20, 000 to open up and operate the shop with other new investments identified. The capital investment will be considered when the current business performs well and shows signs of return on investment. There should be a good return to guarantee that the proposed expansion will also do well. Many other factors will be considered including the university management on the same idea and the availability of resources for expansion.

The company will have to contribute back to the society through corporate social responsibility strategy. It will purchase books for the library and help in giving out some bursaries to needy students. Through employing students as interns, this means that the company starts its corporate social responsibility as soon as it begins.

Bibliography

BBC News. *GM Tomato 'May Boost Health'* Accessed on 6th January 2011
from<http://news.bbc.co.uk/1/hi/sci/tech/7694087.stm>

Don, H., Mowen, M. & Guan L., 2006. *Cost Management: Accounting & Control.* Mason:
South-Western Cangage learning.

Ford, B., Bornstein, J. & Pruitt P., 2007, *Ernst and Young business plan guide,* New Jersey:
John Wiley & Sons Inc.

Jae S. & Siegel J., 2009, *Budgeting Basics and Beyond,* New Jersey: John Wiley & sons Inc.

Kloper, 2006, *Marketing: fresh perspectives,* Cape Town: Longman publishers Ltd.

Kurtz, D., 2007, Contemporary *Marketing,* New York: Nelson education Ltd.

Mayes T., & Mortimore, S., 2001, *Making the most of HACCP: Learning from other's
experience,* Abington: Woodhead Publishing Ltd.

Peri, H., & Pakroo, P., 2008, *The small business start-up kit,* 5th ed., California: Delta
Printing Solution Inc.

Stevens, 1993, *Market analysis: Assessing your business opportunities,* Binghamton: The
Haworth Press Inc.

UK National Statistics, Accessed on 6th January 2011 from <http://www.statistics.gov.uk>

Appendix 1

Photos of food sold

Purple tomatoes

British blackberries

Tomato puree

Appendix 2: Economic graphs

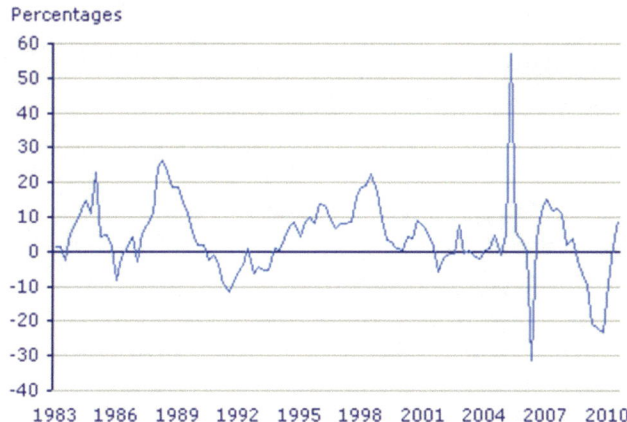

Source: Business investment in UK (http://www.statistics.gov.uk/cci/nugget.asp?id=258)

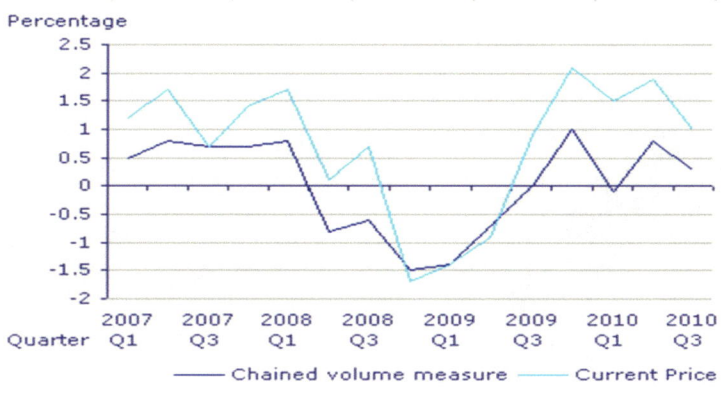

Source: Consumer spending (http://www.statistics.gov.uk/cci/nugget.asp?id=11)